Social Media For Real Estate Agents & Realtors

Real Estate Internet Marketing- Using Social Networking to Grow Your Real Estate Business Fast

Dream Street Investments, Inc.

1

Table of Contents

Introduction Into Social Media

Social media *is* the way of the future! Real Estate Agents and "Realtors" using the power of social media and social networking can grow their real estate business very quickly.

What is Social Media? It is simply one of the best ways to connect with a large amount of people online. A virtual meeting place of sorts.

Traditional Real Estate Marketing Vs. Marketing Via Social Media:
In the past, door knocking and walking the neighborhoods was one of the best ways to reach potential buyers and sellers and grab their attention in hopes they would list or buy a home through you. This is still a good form of marketing; however it can take 3-6 hours or more to reach only 20 to 30 homeowners. With the click of a mouse, you can literally reach hundreds and thousands of potential buyers and sellers when using social media and social networking internet sites.

Every Real Estate agent knows that nearly 90% of buyers and sellers begin their search online, if you are not one of those internet suave agents that they find online, you too will be losing out on 90% of your potential business.

These are staggering but true numbers; and in itself an excellent reason to get yourself positioned online now. Learning the internet marketing curve is not that complicated, but like all marketing sources it takes consistency to be highly effective. However, with consistency you can rapidly boost your workload and your profit!!

We would like to commend you on looking toward the future of your Real Estate business and learning these must-have social media and internet marketing tools now. The internet and online searching is not going away, so now is the time to take action.

Imagine a steady pipeline of real estate business coming to you via email, or facebook, twitter, blogs, and on and on.... Wouldn't you like to log on to your email and see you have 5, 10, 20, or even 30 new prospects that have contacted you and requested information from you? How long do you think it would take through traditional real estate marketing to achieve this amount of potential clients? The best part is most internet marketing doesn't cost you a dime!!

This is how wonderful the internet can be for you and your real estate business! In this book you will learn how to use twitter, facebook, linkedin, WordPress, myspace, expert marketing techniques and ways to properly market your own website for leads, and so much more…

Social media in simple terms is a way to connect online or on the go. Nowadays; nearly 95% of your potential clients, "i.e. Buyers and Sellers" have a cell phone and internet connection and regularly search on the internet while out looking at properties. There are even apps that many buyers have downloaded onto their cell phones that provide them with all the local open houses in the area, available properties, and even Real Estate agents in the local area.

Once you learn how to harness the power of using social media, your real estate business will grow very rapidly! You will be ahead of your local competition as they are all scrambling to learn these techniques.

Successful internet marketing Real Estate agents sometimes receive 10-30 leads daily or more! Real Estate has always been a numbers game. Remember, the more contacts you make = the more clients you will get = the more successful closed transactions you will have! Imagine receiving 10-30 leads daily to sift through, this is amazing!! We have never in the past been able to reach out and connect with potential buyers and sellers like we can by using social networking and internet marketing!! The best part of social media and social networking is that it is very cheap and most times

10

free!! We do have to invest our time, however wouldn't it be great to send out your newsletter in less than 5 minutes to thousands of people!! No more postage to pay for or walking the neighborhoods; and most people have their email accessible via their cell phone!! What an amazing way to reach our farm!

Farming should always be the foundation for your business! Top Real Estate Agents farm year round for new business. Using social media and social networking sites just makes it much easier for us to farm to a vast population quickly.

Now, how do we begin our journey to learning social media, internet marketing and the tools to make our real estate business thrive? Many agents tell us, "I don't know where to begin, there is so much to do"! Do not be overwhelmed with the things you hear, the internet is very friendly! In this book we will take you through the steps to getting you signed up with all the major places you need to be found online to boost your Real Estate business.

One of the key components in successful social media marketing implementation is building "social authority". What does this mean? Social authority is developed when an individual establishes themselves as an "expert" in their given field or area, thereby becoming an influencer in that field or area of expertise. **You** want to be the authority and area expert and by marketing your services online you will be the one they find and contact for their next real estate transaction!

As a result of social media –today, consumers are as likely – or more likely – to make buying decisions based on what they read and see in platforms we call "social" but only if presented by someone they have come to trust. That is why a purposeful and carefully designed social media strategy has become an integral part of any complete and directed marketing plan but must also be designed using newer "authority building" techniques.

The one thing to always remember about social media and internet marketing is the internet is always changing! New content "i.e. Blogs, articles, websites, etc." are always being added to the internet so it is very important to add new content about you and your real estate services on a regular basis. Dedicate a fixed time each week you will work on your blogs, facebook, twitter, etc. Then, STICK TO IT!!! Your followers and friends online will come to look for your new material and information you are posting and if you do not post regularly they will not want to hear what you have to say, at least online that is. If you are going to work on your internet marketing two times a week, pencil it in your schedule and remain committed to it. Once you are setup, it becomes very easy to handle. We will show you tips and tricks to post your information in one place and have it shared simultaneously on all of your social media websites such as facebook, twitter, linkedin, myspace, Google, yahoo, etc with the click of the mouse!!! Your potential clients will think you spent years on the internet, and this builds there trust with you and your services even more!

The internet is an open playground for Real Estate agents & Realtors! Congratulations on taking your first steps toward ruling the internet!! Let's begin to create you into internet marketing kings and queens!! Let the fun begin!!

Chapter 1

Social Media For Real Estate Agents & Realtors

Real Estate Internet Marketing- Using Social Networking to Grow Your Real Estate Business Fast

Welcome to the world of Social Media for Real Estate Agents and Realtors. This book will teach you how to become a top internet marketer for your real estate business. Learn how to unleash the power of the internet and watch your Real Estate business soar to new heights. Learn how to find clients from twitter, facebook, myspace, linkedin, yelp, learn tools to start receiving free leads from your website (stop paying for website leads), how to get your website increased in google and the search engines, place free classified ads advertising your services, submit free article submissions promoting you and your website, blogs and so much more...

14

Nearly 95% of real estate professionals across the US have a website, but less than 5% of real estate professionals actually get valuable leads from their website. Stop paying for leads from other websites out there, learn how to turn your website into a money making venue for your business. 87% of buyers and investors start looking on the internet before they even contact a realtor, learn how to capture those buyers and turn them into customers. You will learn about SEO (Search Engine Optimization) and how this will make your potential customers find your website. It's a must have to have a website in the real estate profession, but the best website does you no good if your website can not be found!!!

Learn valuable tools to get found on google, yahoo, Bing, AOL, and other search engines so customers can find you today! Learn how to create blogs to promote people to your website and learn about your services. Find places to place free ads offering your services. Use craigslist to promote your services. Join valuable networks and connect with other real estate people, buyers, and investors. Make videos and upload them onto youtube, myspace, and more to promote your services.
Install google analytics to track how many visitors are coming to your website and where they are coming from!
Turn your website into a lead generating tool today!

Social media marketing which is known as **SMO or Social Media Optimization.** Social media marketing benefits Real Estate Agents, Realtors, and individuals by providing an additional channel for customer support; it is a great means to gain a vast amount of customers and competitive insight quickly, and a method of managing your reputation online. Key factors of social media marketing is that it ensures its success and its relevance to the customer. The old adage "What's in it for me!" applies, when you provide information online that is valuable to buyers and sellers, they will listen and listen well. And your Real Estate Business will grow because of it, many times very, very quickly! To get buyers and sellers to listen to what you have to say online includes providing them with information that is usable to them. No one really cares if you are the top agent in xyz realty or you sold 30 million dollars in real estate, they want to know what you can do for them. It is always important to express your skills and expert knowledge on the information you post online and in all marketing avenues, however you will obtain a greater response from people when you provide them with relevant information that can help them. This book will show you how to do just that and much, much more. A strong social media foundation serves as a stand or platform in which you can centralize all your information and direct customers straight to your website via other social media channels, such as articles, blogs, facebook, twitter, Google buzz, Activerain, Trulia, Zillow, press release publications, and a wealth of other social media sites.

The most popular social media websites include:

Facebook, YouTube, Linkedin, Twitter, Myspace, Reddit, Delicious, Trulia, Zillow, Activerain, Bigger pockets, Blogger, and many more!

Social networking websites have taken the internet by storm and there are countless ones to join and network on. In this book we are going to touch on all the main social media and social networking websites that are great for Real Estate Agents and Realtors.

Let the Social Media Journey Begin!

Summary of topics to be covered in this Social Media Book:

1. SEO (Search Engine Optimization) Learn tools to adjust your website to be found easier in google and the search engines
2. Submit your website to the search engines to get your website found online fast
3. Using Twitter to becoming a networking powerhouse for you & your website
4. Using Facebook to generate more clients and connect with others to offer your services, Advertise all your open houses on the facebook events-this generates tons of people to your open houses
5. Placing free ads offering your services and sending them to your website
6. Blogs-Blogging is an excellent way to promote you and your business and to send many people to your website
7. Place free ads on Craigslist offering your services
8. Write free articles about what you have to offer and interesting things about your community to drive people to your website

9. Install an auto-responder if you don't have one for your emails so people get an instant response once they have visited your website

10. Join Industry networks & network with others in your   community

11. Create videos of you and your services and place them on

   Youtube, myspace, facebook, and more sending people to your website

12. Install google analytics so you can track the amount of people visiting your website and where they found you from

13. Offer your customers free tools and tips on your website to capture their email address and then respond to them in a timely manner

Chapter 2

SEO (Search Engine Optimization) and Why You NEED It for your Website & Social Media Networking Success!

What is search engine optimization?

Search engine optimization is the process of making a website and its content highly relevant for both search engines and searchers. SEO "search engine optimization" includes implementing technical tasks to make it easier for search engines to find and index your website or websites by adding the appropriate keywords and meta-tags which will increase your website rank in search engines such as Google, yahoo, bing, and the many other search engines that exist, as well as marketing-focused tasks to make a site more appealing to users.

It sounds very complicated and technical, but there are some basics that anyone with a website can do to increase your websites ability to show up in the search engines. Current statistics say that the average person searching the internet only views up to the first 5 websites that come up for that search term, this means if you can not position your website high enough in Google, yahoo, and the other search engines that most of your potential customers will be visiting someone else's real estate website, thus becoming their client and not yours. You want to show up in the search engines so your potential customers can find you and find you first! Always attempt to make your website clean and easy to navigate, however also very keyword heavy, especially on the Home page of your website. There are many free tools on the internet to help you come up with your keywords and meta-tags, our best recommendation is to imagine you were a buyer and type in searches in the search engine that you would look for, then you have basically come up with you keep words, do the same for sellers. Then, place these terms in your home page, this will greatly increase your website ranking and most likely get your website closer to becoming #1 in Google and the other search engines.

The Internet has profoundly transformed the way people learn about and shop for products and especially Real Estate. Ten years ago, "Realtors" reached their consumers through phone books, print advertising, and other traditional marketing methods. Today, buyers and sellers start shopping for their next Real Estate agent and house by looking on the Internet, in the search engines, the blogosphere, and social media sites. More people look online in yellowpages.com than actually pick up a traditional phone book these days. In order to remain competitive and set yourself apart from the pack, your Real Estate website needs to be found online by the consumers already searching for the services that you sell. Doing these simple steps will make your website and all your social media marketing efforts shine above the rest of your competitors.

Chapter 3

MARKETING YOUR OWN WEBSITE

FOR SUCCESS!

95% of Realtors have their own website, 100% of Real estate agents ***should have one***!   With that said, less than 5% of Realtors know how to market their website effectively. Marketing your website does take persistence, however the rewards are astounding and definitely worth the little bit of time you invest into developing an effective website. When considering which website to choose, you will want to make sure that you will have these options available:

1. You can customize the website to your own needs- even if it comes with a template, you will want to be able to customize it to your specific needs

2. Make sure you can enter all meta-tags and keywords so your website can be indexed quickly with all the search engines

3. One of the best things to do for your website, yet very few Realtors do this is to add an autoresponder to your website. An autoresponder is when a potential client leaves their email address and your system immediately emails them information. This also frees you up from having to sit by the computer waiting for potential buyers and sellers to contact you, plus it appears you are immediately responding to your online customer. Statistics say that online potential clients expect to be contacted within less than 2 minutes or they will move onto another website to find what they are looking for.

4. Make sure the website company provides local school information and local community links with all their templates as this is crucial information buyers and sellers will be looking for.

Currently 89% of people searching the internet do it from a desktop computer or laptop; however this is about to change very rapidly. By the year 2013, local experts say that 96% of people searching the internet will be doing this from their cell phones, mobile readers, or some type of portable viewing device. There are billions of websites on the internet and currently less than 50,000 are formatted for viewing on cell phones and portable devices properly. All big name companies such as Nike, Pepsi, and many more are now doing this; however in the next couple of years, this will be a standard for anyone with a website! Beat out your competition and get your website optimized for viewing on mobile devices as soon as possible. Imagine that 96% of buyers are driving around town and looking on their cell phone for all the local realtors or properties for sale in the area and your website comes up, however it isn't viewing properly on these mobile devices or cell phones, you will lose this customer almost instantly! We recommend doing this once you have optimized your website to capture all of these buyers and sellers.

Chapter 4
Powerful Marketing: Offering Something FREE to your Website Visitors Such as Tips, Updates, Newsletters, or Ebooks

Many visitors, especially buyers do not like to immediately give you their email address for fear that they will feel pressured. Offer them something for free and they only have to leave their name and email address to receive it, it's a great way to capture their email so you may continue following up with them and turn that lead into a transaction!!! Provide valuable content on your website to keep visitors coming back!! Offering some free tips or even an ebook on buying or selling is a great way to capture their email! This has worked excellent for many Realtors we know! Give it a try and you will be amazed at how many people actually go on your website and now leave you their email address and contact information!

Chapter 5

Businesses must get found online by the consumers searching for their products and services in the:

Search Engines

Blogosphere

Social Media

There are two kinds of search results: paid results and organic (or natural) results.

Paid results are those listings that require a fee for the search engines to list their link for particular keywords. The most widely used form of paid listing is Pay Per Click (PPC), where you pay each time someone clicks on the link in your advertisement. The price increases with the competitiveness of the keyword.

Chapter 6

Organic results are gathered by search engines' web crawlers and ranked according to relevance to search terms. This relevance is calculated by criteria such as extent of keyword match and number of links into that website. Ranking in the organic search results is better because not only is it FREE, but research shows that people click on the organic results 75% of the time and paid results only 25% of the time.

Google and the other search engines rank websites in search engine results pages according to relevance to the search terms. This relevance is calculated by looking at both on-page factors such as the content on your site and off-page factors in the form of inbound links to your website. Off-page factors are the biggest influencers in your website's ranking in search engine results.

Find Keywords
STEP 1: Pick your keywords for your website

Search Volume – Given two different keyword phrases, optimize for the one with the larger number of searches.

Relevance – Choose keywords that your target market is using to describe and search for your products and services.

Difficulty or Competition – Consider your chances for ranking on the first page of Google for that keyword phrase.

Look at the sites ranked in those first 10 slots, their authority and relevance to search terms, and gage if you will be able to overtake them to secure a spot on that first page.

STEP 2: On-Page SEO

Place keywords in the page title, URL, headings, and page text. This definitely helps you website get indexed better in the search engines!!

Optimize your page description for maximum click-through-rate when your site ranks in Google searches.

Place keywords in other "invisible" places on your site, including meta-keyword tags and alt-text on images.

STEP 3: Off-Page SEO

Build more inbound links from other sites into yours. Each link serves as a recommendation or a reference to tell the search engines that your site is a quality site.

Build more links within context, i.e. those with valuable keywords in the link anchor text (the text that is hyperlinked to your site). Link anchor text provides context for the search engines to understand what your site is about.

Build more links from trusted websites. Just as references from well-respected friends and experts offer more value, so do links from trusted and well-respected websites.

Link-building tips:

Submit your website to directories like the Yahoo!
Directory and Business.com

Communicate with others in your industry through blogs
and other social media

Create compelling tools (such as an interesting calculator)
and content (via a blog, for example)

STEP 4: Measure & Analyze

Track number of inbound links, keyword rank over time
and compared to competition.

Measure real business results: number of visitors, leads,
and customers from SEO. Install google analytics to your
website to track how many visitors you are receiving and
where they are coming from.

Once you have done some of these things to improve your
website, I would recommend to have one of the free

website graders on the internet score your website to see where you can improve your search engine visibility.

Here are some websites you can go to:
www.websitegrader.com
www.reviewmyweb.com

Submit your website to the Search Engines: Now that you have tuned up your website, you need to submit it to the search engines.

Even if your website has been in the search engines before, you will need to resubmit it for the search engines to crawl and analyze your website. You should have you website submitted every month if possible. There are literally billions of websites on the internet and you need to constantly submit to them to be found, also as you do the other tools in this guide you will watch your website start moving toward the first page of search results greatly increasing the amount of visitors you have on your website. You can do this manually, however it does take time or you can pay someone to submit your site to multiple search engines for you. There are companies that do it freely in exchange for placing their link on your homepage.

Here are a couple of companies you can use:
www.google.com/addurl/
www.**submit**express.com/**submit**.html

www.addme.com
www.freewebsubmission.com/

And there are many more sites to submit your site to, just google search submit my site to the search engines and you can find more companies

Getting your website and content found on Google and all the other search engines is the key to your success! One way to have your website, blogs, facebook, twitter, and social networking websites be found is by link building. There are websites out there that charge a fee for link building services; however, you never need to pay for these services. Google and all the search engines rank websites by content and the links to the websites, with the tools we provide you in this book, when you connect all of your different social media and social networking websites together automatically builds links to your website.

Search engines will basically score your website and content by the amount of links going to and from your website, the more website links you have coming to your website, the lower your traffic ranking will be. Usually a higher number would seem to be best, but not in traffic ranking, the lower the number is, the better your website is rated!

Chapter 7

Also, link text helps get your website ranked better in the search engines. This is simply having certain words in a blog or article that are relevant words "such as buying a home" and those words link to your website. The search engines will see this and recognize your website as somewhere buyers can go to get information about buying a home. Google and many of the top search engines rank websites very highly for using links and link text. This will get your website closer to the top of the search results when people are searching on the internet.

Get Found Online: Blogs

What is a blog? A blog, or weblog, is a website that allows for regularly posted content or articles. Blogging is Inbound Marketing-Placing interesting content about you or your services out on the web where they will choose to find you.

Blogging helps with SEO

Blogging helps with social news and networking sites

Blogging is permission centric

The conversation has already started… it's time that you're aware of it and develop a strategy for engaging in it and using it for marketing your business and services.

How to Get Found Online: Blogs

1: Read other blogs that pertain to your area or real estate market, there are blogs so specific they even talk about specific housing tracts and events in the area

Search for other blogs in your industry using Technorati.com or BlogSearch.Google.com.

Read and subscribe to blogs via RSS (Really Simple Syndication) or email – RSS allows users to subscribe anonymously and consume content however they want. It also records what you write and blog about and sends that to the search engines constantly.

2: Comment on other people's blogs

Contribute to the conversation via a comment

Increase the value of the article – share an example, add a point, add a useful link, disagree, ask a question. Why? When you engage in the community, then more and more people will read it and want to talk to you

This is also a great way to create links back to your website and this will increase your website ranking and the amount of visitors to your website seeking your services.

Add a Blog to Your Own Website

You may want to provide tips and updates for your local real estate market on your blog, as we have said before; you can literally blog about almost anything.

In every blog you do make sure to reference your own website and contact information.

Install an Auto-Responder for your Email

When people go to your website and would like to contact via your website, they usually fill in their information and hit send. You will then receive the email, but as we all know how very important we are, we may not be sitting in front of the computer at the time it comes in. An email auto-responder will email them immediately letting them know that you will be contacting them shortly. Potential clients love this as they feel that you have responded to them immediately, it builds trust and will help you secure those internet leads you receive.

Get Found Online: Social Media

What is social media? Media (content that is published) with a social (anyone can add to and share it) component. Social media is like a business networking reception without the constraints of time and space.

Social Media is Inbound Marketing

Social media helps with SEO

Social media promotes your blog

Social media is permission centric

Some of the Top Social Media websites are facebook, twitter, myspace, linkedin, squidoo, and there are so many more. We are going to talk about facebook, twitter, and myspace but, do not stop there, there are literally millions of social networking sites out there. Join as many as you want to, the more you join the more it will increase the marketing of your services and your website to attack visitors.

One excellent social network for real estate is the Foreclosure Network, go to www.foreclosurecleanupnetwork.com and join-it's free and only takes a couple of minutes to register and you are instantly networking with other real estate professionals, buyers, investors, contractors, and more.

Chapter 8
How you can use Twitter to Grow your Real Estate Business
www.twitter.com

Here are some of the topics we are going to cover:
What is Twitter?
Why is it valuable?
How does it work?
How should a business get started?
What does it make possible?
Your fears and concerns
And Much More…

What is twitter?

Twitter is a completely mobile way of interacting with a huge audience; you can interact through your mobile phone or on the internet. People type short messages, less than 140 characters about interesting topics and network between each other.

Why is it valuable? Brand your name out through tons of people at one time for free-twitter costs nothing but time!

Twitter has 160 million registered users and has 90 Million tweets per day!!

Here is a great website to learn all about twitter and what it can do for you:
http://business.twitter.com/twitter101

Twitter allows you to engage more deeply with consumers and markets in strategic and powerful ways.

So what does Twitter do for businesses?

Twitter is a communication platform that helps businesses stay connected to their customers. As a business, you can use it to quickly share information with people interested in your company or using your services and build relationships with customers   and other people who care about you or your company.

As an individual user, you can use Twitter to tell a company (or anyone else) that you've had a great—or disappointing—experience with their business, offer product ideas, and learn about great offers.

So how does it work?

Twitter lets you write and read messages of up to 140 characters or less in length, including all punctuation and spaces. The messages are public and you decide what sort of messages you want to receive—Twitter being a recipient driven information network. In addition, you can send and receive Twitter messages, or tweets, equally well from your desktop or your mobile phone.

So how do businesses use Twitter?

Twitter connects you to your customers right now, in a way that was never before possible.

*With twitter you can: Build your network fast, access better professional relationships, have faster knowledge-sharing!

Value Twitter can be for you & your business:

    Visibility   Relevance   Relationships
    Social capital   Community   Ideas Trust
        Marketing   Networking
    Customer service Drive Traffic to your website

What's in it for you?
    INFLUENCE-Attracting attention to yourself and your website!!!

Before you post your first message

Before you get started, it's important to understand that on Twitter, people choose to view your updates by searching for specific keywords or by following your account.

This recipient-controlled model means that if you are compelling to people on Twitter, they'll choose to view your updates. The reverse is also true—people may choose to un-follow you just as easily.

Dry, boring feeds rarely draw many people. Successful Twitter business accounts, though, can take many forms. They may be personal and chatty or they might even have mostly automated information. But no matter the style, the key is to post messages that your followers will find compelling.

Tip: Help people understand what to expect from your Twitter account by posting a little description in your Bio.

So making your posts on Twitter interesting is key, but what are you going to post about? That depends on your goals. Do you want to build deeper relationships? Or do you want to provide more responsive and immediate customer service?

You can meet several communication goals simultaneously by thinking about your Twitter account as a friendly information booth or place to chat.

It's a place for people to ask you spontaneous questions of all kinds—a spot to share intriguing company insights they might find interesting. Tweeting often can help build valuable relationships.

Regardless of how you plan on using Twitter, you should figure out how to integrate it with your existing communication channels.

To get a sense of what Twitter can do for your business, spend a little time listening in on the conversations happening right now (you can use Twitter search whether or not you have an account). Listening will help you quickly learn what people are saying about you or your company, and it will also give you a feel for the flow of conversations on Twitter. In addition, it can give you insight into how other companies handle Twitter exchanges

Once you've got a sense of how you want to engage on Twitter, you're ready to dive in.

Jump in and get started today!

If you haven't yet signed up for an account, it's easy, and it takes just a few minutes. Here's how to get started:

Sign up

Go to the sign up page, www.twitter.com and fill out the four fields. If you're creating a company account, use the "Full name" field to type in your company name. That'll help people find your company or team on Twitter. (You can add your own name in the Bio field, as described below.) If you are not part of a real estate team, then I would recommend using your personal name, not your company's name.

The Username is the name by which you'll be known on Twitter, for real estate professionals I highly recommend this to be your name. This will promote your name more and more for people to remember you as a professional in their area and someone they can call on when they want to utilize your services or recommend you to someone.

After you've signed up, the site will walk you through a couple of screens to help you find people on Twitter you know or might be interested in.

Fill out your information

Before you do anything else, click Settings to get a page where you can fill out a few more details to help people recognize your company. Most of the fields are self-explanatory. But pay special attention to the Bio, which gives you quite a bit of space to write about yourself; this is a great place to list information about you and what you have to offer, always make sure to include your website, email information, and phone number, too.

Before you leave Settings, check out the Picture tab, you should definitely add a photo of yourself as this helps the other twitter people to easily remember and recognize you more. On the Design tab, you can upload a background image for your Twitter home page and change the page colors to your choice.

Find highly relevant people and companies to follow.

Whether or not you chose to follow anyone in the sign-up process, now's a good time to search for people and companies of specific interest to you. Use the search box on your Twitter home page to look not only for people talking about your company, brands and products, but also for partners and mentions of key terms in your sector. When you find interesting messages, consider following those accounts. No need to worry about the number of people you're following—just follow a few whose updates you really want to read, say hello and let conversations grow. Go to the Find People section and type whatever search term you would like to enter to find people.

Post your first message

This is where the fun begins. On your Twitter home page, in the box at the top, it says "What are you doing?" Type in a message; whatever you would like to type in there. When you've finished typing what you want to say, hit Update to post it (pressing Enter won't do the trick). There you go, you've done it-you've sent your first tweet.

If you chose to skip the step during setup of searching for people, you should do this now. People will not see your messages unless you have people following you, add as many people and businesses as you would like, the more the better. People are very friendly on twitter and when you follow them, most of the time the start following you. Good luck and get tweeting!!

Twitter is a great way for real estate professionals to become well known in their area, take advantage of that!!!

Get Tweeting today!!

Chapter 9
Real Estate and Facebook-Unleash the Power of Facebook & Use it to Grow your Real Estate Business Fast!
www.facebook.com

Facebook is another excellent website for networking for real estate professionals. Make sure your site that you use for your facebook contains appropriate content as your website would. You will be able to connect with customers once you started networking.

**Facebook has more than 500 million active users registered and over 50% of users log on to it at least once a day!!! And more than 150 Million active users currently access Facebook through their mobile devices. People spend more than 700 BILLION minutes per month on Facebook! If that isn't enough reason to get your business on facebook, than I don't know what is!!!

So let's get started....

Facebook is the #2 website that people log onto the internet currently and this is surely to grow in the near future. Many people are even setting the home page to facebook as their home page when the internet browser opens. YOU MUST embrace Facebook, if you do not, your competition will have a very large advantage over you! Next, we are going to take you step by step to get your facebook account setup. If you have a facebook account already and just need to learn how to start using facebook to market yourself and your services, we still recommend reading this entire chapter on facebook.

First you will want to go to www.facebook.com and sign up; it only takes a few minutes. Then, create your profile if you don't have one already. Add your pictures and tell about yourself completely and include your website, email, and phone number so people can contact you. **One important thing to remember is facebook only allows users to have one profile, yes this is right.**

DO NOT HAVE MORE THAN ONE ACCOUNT ON FACEBOOK, if they find out you do have more than one account they can ban you permanently from facebook. This does not mean one account for business and one account for personal use, it means one account period. Also, direct marketing in your profile repeatedly is a form of spam, we will teach you how to create business pages and you can aggressively market your real estate services here. You can also get a custom domain name once you have received at least 25 people to "like" your business page. As a real estate professional, many people will find you on facebook but may want to call you and speak to you personally. Keep your facebook professional as these are people you will want to business with. You can easily have family and friends connected with you as well as keep your facebook appearing professional to the public by setting up your settings properly and not allowing your family postings to show on your facebook wall. Next, you will want to connect with people you already know, you can important your email address book and it will tell you of other people that are already on facebook that you can connect with. You can easily search for people, too. Go to the search bar at the top and type in what you are searching for, "for example physicians Los Angeles", it will bring up all the people that reference this in their profiles, then just send them a request to join. You can also grow very quickly by joining groups as some groups have thousands of people in just one group, then when you post something on facebook, all of these members of this group as well as all of your friends will see what you have posted. This is a very powerful marketing source and the reach of potential customers is huge.

Now-Start Connecting with Huge Groups of People

Many people are already on facebook and do not know that facebook has discussion areas, entire huge groups of people discussing different topics. Go to the search bar and type in discussions.

An entire page will come up where you can search by people, pages, groups, and more. Search out the people you would like to add. Then go back and search out real estate groups, investors, local shopping groups, etc. You can add as many groups as you want, just remember the more people and groups you add the more people you will be marketing to simultaneously when you post information. Now that you've added people and groups, these people will all see everything you add to your facebook page and it will encourage them to come back to your site more often and see what you are up to. Another really quick way for all of your friends to see your face on facebook literally daily is to "like" what they post. Just like when you post information such as status updates, comments, links, photos, videos, etc. – you can click that you like it. Every time you do this it brings up your face and the link to your profile! This is one very fast way to always show up on your friend's facebook wall! Give it a try, posting on facebook is very, very easy. Just type something simple and update your status, all of your friends will see and read this. When first starting out on facebook, we recommend spending at least 20 minutes a day to add new friends and post information. If you set a goal to invest at least 20 minutes a day, before you know it you will have a huge following of friends and every single time you post something they will all see your new post and remind them of you and your real estate services you have to offer.

Chapter 10
Creating Facebook Business Pages-One of the Best Marketing Sources for Facebook-Supercharge Your Real Estate Marketing with Facebook Business Pages

What is a Facebook Business Page?
Business accounts are designed for individuals who only want to use the site to administer Pages and their ad campaigns, better known as a facebook business page. For this reason, business accounts do not have the same functionality as personal accounts. Business accounts have limited access to information on the site. An individual with a business account can view all the Pages and Social Ads that they have created, however they will not be able to view the profiles of users on the site or other content on the site that does not live on the Pages they administer. The benefit of this is that you can create a complete marketing channel devoted to your local area, real estate career, or whatever you are looking to market and the person who creates the business page is completely confidential. In

addition, business accounts cannot be found in search and cannot send or receive friend requests.

If you are a public figure, we highly recommend you create a Page on Facebook in addition to your personal profile. You should continue to use your personal profile to connect with your family, friends and the people who are important to you and use your Facebook Business Page as a public profile to connect with your fans, supporters and followers.

You can get started creating your Facebook Business Page with these simple steps:

Login into your existing Facebook Account or create an account. Once you have logged in click here: http://www.facebook.com/page.

Next you will need to choose if you want to market by local area or brand. You can not change this once the page is created, so choose accurately. For Real Estate, you will usually want to choose local. Then, choose your category.

Congratulations, that quickly you just created a business page on facebook! The best part is you want to choose a title name for your page that is frequently searched, you can create this page to have a custom domain name dedicated to that title once you receive at least 25 people to "like" you new page.

Next, upload a picture for your page, this will become your profile picture for this page and it will be the first thing they see whenever you post on this business page. Then, add some links and information to the page. Once you have done this, you will want to "suggest" your business page to all your friends to "like it". You do this by clicking on the button that says suggest to friends, then click on all your friends pictures and hit ok. In the click of the mouse you just send a request to all your friends to come check out your new business page, For traditional facebook profiles, you are limited to 5000 friends but business pages are unlimited and they come up excellent in the search engines. Before you know it you will have well over 25 people that have "liked" your page, once you have attained the 25 "liked" requirement, you can log into your profile and request to have the custom domain name. Then, you will want to share this page on Google, yahoo, and all the search engines to be indexed quickly so it starts coming up in the search engines and more people can find you.

Here is the website link to learn more in detail about how to setup a custom business page, remember it is

very simple and can be done in less than 20 minutes most of the time.
http://www.facebook.com/FacebookPages

Try to make this business page interesting, add pictures, links, and post regularly to it. Before you know it you will have this business page coming up top in the search engines with great links back to your own website and all your contact information available so potential buyers, sellers, and investors can contact you.

Now that you have you facebook profile created and made your own facebook business page, go back to your profile and add some widgets. One very good widget is the profile badge, when you create a profile badge it will give you custom html code, just click on it and copy the entire contents of the html code, then go to any blogs or websites you may have and you can paste this code directly in the site, it gives all people reading your blogs and websites a direct link to your facebook page. Plus it helps create great back links to your website increasing your personal business website performance.

Many of your buyers and sellers are very internet suave and have apps that they use to access

facebook. To learn more about mobile apps, here is the website link:
http://developers.facebook.com/docs/guides/mobile/

If you would like to create your own app for facebook, here is the website link:
http://developers.facebook.com/docs/guides/canvas/

People love apps, there is literally an app for nearly everything you can imagine, grab hold of this concept of apps as it will be growing very rapidly.

One app we find very user friendly and good for real estate professionals is called Roostapp, there website is:
http://www.facebook.com/RoostApp
We are not affiliated with or endorse roostapp, we personally just find this one very easy to use.

This can help you create very dynamic facebook business pages and is geared for the real estate agent.

There are many more, to search for other apps go to:
http://apps.facebook.com/marketplace/

Chapter 11
How to Create Community Pages of Facebook?

Community Pages on Facebook

Community Pages are a new type of Facebook Page dedicated to a topic or experience that is owned collectively by the community connected to it. Just like official Pages for businesses, organizations and public figures, Community Pages let you connect with others who share similar interests and experiences.

On each Community Page, you'll be able to learn more about a topic of the community page—whether it's local real estate information, things to do in your local area, or learning how to clean foreclosure bank owned properties—and you can see what your friends and others in the Facebook community are saying about this topic. Facebook started these community pages by showing Wikipedia information, but they are also looking for people who are passionate about any of these topics to sign up to contribute to the Community Page.

Here's how it works:

- **Opt-in to new connections:** When you next visit your profile page on Facebook, you'll see a box appear that recommends Pages based on the interests and connections you'd previously added to your profile. You can then either connect to all these Pages by clicking "Link All to My Profile" or choose specific Pages and click you like the page. You can opt to only connect to some of those Pages by going to "Choose Pages Individually" and checking or un-checking specific Pages. Once you make your choice of pages you want, any text you'd previously had for the current city, hometown, education and work, and likes and interests sections of your profile will be replaced by links to these Pages. You can also use features and applications such as "Notes", status updates or Photos to share more about yourself.
- **How to Add connections:** If you want to add more connections to your profile, just click "Like" on any Facebook Page. This use to be called "Become a Fan" for Business Pages but it has been replaced with a "Like" button. Clicking "Like" on a Facebook Business Page or

Community Pages adds that connection in the related area of your profile's Info section.

- **How to Manage and Remove Connections:** If you no longer want to connect to a business page or someone's profile any longer, you can remove it from your profile at any point. To do this you can either go to the Business or Community Page itself and select "Unlike" from the bottom left hand column, or you can edit your profile, select the Page and click "Remove" underneath the Page photo. If you want to keep the Page on your profile but you do not want certain people to see it on your profile, here are some ways you can customize it to appear on your page.

- **Feature certain connections:** When you edit your profile, you can choose to feature some of your connections over others. Simply drag and drop your favorite Business Pages or Community pages above or below the fold to dictate which ones are most prominent when friends visit your profile. You can change the order of these pages anytime. If you move a Page below the fold, your friends will still be able to see that connection if they click "See More" beside the field.

- **How to Control the Visibility of What Content Appears on your Profile Pages:** Within your Privacy Settings under the Account menu, you have a section called friends, tags and connections. You can adjust each different setting from the drop-down menus beside each field, this lets you determine who can see the different parts of your profile. You can even choose to hide your friend's list; we highly recommend doing this. This way your competitors will not seek you out and start adding your friends and marketing to them.

Keep in mind that Facebook Pages you connect to *are* public. You can control which friends are able to see the connections listed on your profile, but you may still show up on Pages you're connected to. If you don't want to show up on those Pages, simply disconnect from them by clicking the "Unlike" link in the bottom left column of the Page. You always decide what connections to make and you can change them at anytime.

Strategic Marketing on Facebook-Creating Facebook Paid Ads

These are similar to google adwords where you pay for the advertising; however they have very reasonable rates that I would not over look this as a way of advertising. You ads will display on facebook users profiles, you only pay people click on your ads or by the amount of profiles per thousand impressions in shows up on.

Here are some links to facebook advertising:

http://www.facebook.com/advertising/

http://www.facebook.com/marketing

http://www.facebook.com/adsmarketing/

You can even specify your marketing ads to only show up in your geographical area, specific group of individuals you want to market to, and by the age of the users. Facebook pay per click advertising is a very powerful marketing tool to use. You can also specify how much you would like to spend daily or monthly to advertise on facebook. For example, say you wanted your facebook ad to appear on all members' profiles in your local city, age 25 and older, between the hours of 4pm to 10pm, you can do this. You can even set it to have a daily budget of $5 per day, which is approximately $150 per month. For this $150 per month, you will be seen every day on the users profile pages to the right with your picture ad linking to your website showcasing your services. This is one way to reach literally thousands of people without having to hardly do anything once your ad is setup.

Chapter 12
Real Estate Marketing, Networking and Myspace-How to Grow your business on myspace

MySpace has nearly 130 million monthly active users around the globe

MySpace has more than 70 million total unique users in the US

Myspace was one of the first social media giants to grow to outstanding numbers, facebook has actually surpassed myspace, however you still have 70 million potential customers out there to market to!

MySpace is all over the news and all over computer screens across America and beyond. In November of 2005, MySpace had 26.7 million users estimated. Just one year later, an estimated 128 million people were using MySpace, the site that according to Wikipedia "attracts new registrations at a rate of 230,000 per day". And although teens may appear to be more hip to

MySpace lingo, an October 2006 report by comScore Media Metrix notes that **"more than half of all MySpace visitors are now age 35 or older."**

Getting Started on Myspace:

First go to www.myspace.com and register and set up your account and profile. Once again, include your picture, website, email, phone number and what you have to offer your potential clients.

Next, search for friends, collegues, former clients, and potential clients in the browse people search bar and send them friend requests so you can get connected to them. You can also search by occupation and other topics to find friends to connect with.

How to Post Events on Myspace:

You can post events such as open houses and more on the more tab, here's the link:

http://event.myspace.com/index.cfm?fuseaction=events

You must be logged into your account to do this. Once you post events, it will show up in there updates wall and you can also send a message to all of your friends announcing the event. Here is another great FREE way to advertise your open houses, buyer seminars, seller seminars, foreclosure tours, or whatever else you would like to advertise your event for.

FREE Myspace Classified Ads:

Place free classified ads offering your real estate services on myspace, these ads can be seen across the US.

Here's the link:

http://www.classifieds.myspace.com/

Paid Myspace Advertising-How to Create an Ad to show up on Myspace users profiles

Use banner ads to drive traffic to your real estate website. You can even place banners and text ads in your specific area with myspace similar to facebook.

Here is the link:

https://advertise.myspace.com/

You can run banner and text ads for as low as $5 a day and have them only advertise in the areas you want them to, and you can even target by age. This is another great way to market your business and reach thousands to millions of potential customers.

Chapter 13
Google Adwords-Advertise on the 1st page of Google now!

Advertise your business on Google, Google is the giant when it comes to search engines and 85% of all internet searches originate from a Google search. When people are searching for business information or needs, this number goes up dramatically so you will definitely want to market yourself on Google to be found online.

Google adwords is amazing! Even if your website does not come up on the 1st page of Google, when you create an ad on Google adwords, your ad will be displayed on the top or to the right of all the search results.

No matter what your budget, you can display your ads on Google. You will pay only if people click your ads. You can set your own budget upon how much you want to spend, your geographical area, and more.

To get started with Google adwords:
Go to: www.google.com
And type in google adwords to be taken to the signup page.

Chapter 14
Advertising your Real Estate Services on Craiglist:

http://www.craigslist.org/about/sites

Craiglist is a great place to offer your services that is absolutely free! You need to post almost daily, but millions of people look on craigslist everyday!! You can post in several places on craigslist, one place to post ads on is the services category, another top place to advertise in is the real estate for sale or lease categories. You may even want to market in the events section for open houses, or buyer seminars. There are some websites that offer ad creators and if you have an ad in html code, you can simply code and paste this code into the ad you are creating on craigslist to make it stand out more.

Chapter 15
Online Real Estate Directories-Make sure you are listed on ALL the online directories of Real Estate Agents & Professionals in your area

Being listed in all the Real Estate Online Directories is a must-have and it also adds another link to your own business real estate website. We have listed some of the best real estate online directories below:

http://www.instanthomelink.com/
http://www.justrealestate.org/
http://www.epoweredprofessionals.com/
http://www.realtorfinder.com/
http://www.realestateagent.com/
http://www.iqrealestate.com/
http://www.real-estate-directories.com/
http://www.us-realestatedirectory.com/
http://www.onlinerealestatepro.com/
http://www.4-estateagent.com/
http://agentmonster.com/
http://www.homegain.com/find_real_estate_agent/index
http://realestate.yahoo.com/Realtors
http://www.realestateabc.com/
http://www.iqrealestate.com/

Chapter 16
Linkedin-An Excellent Place for All Real Estate Professionals

Linkedin is a place for business professionals and investors to connect and network. It is mainly for business professionals and investors, over 80 Million business users in over 200 countries use linked in to stay in touch and market to one another. It is even available in many different languages such as English, French, German, Italian, Portuguese and Spanish. Many people go on linkedin to also search for industry related jobs and business opportunities.

You will definitely want to create a linkedin profile if you are in the real estate industry! It is very easy to create your profile on linkedin and in minutes you will be up and running. So let's get started!

Go to:
http://www.linkedin.com/

Once you have signed up, add your profile picture and all contact information about yourself. Once again, the way social media is amazing is by the connections you have. Join groups on linkedin once you have completed your profile, there are some groups with as many members as 30,000, sign up for as many groups as you can. When you first join linkedin there is usually a limit to how many groups you can join, once you have started networking you will be able to join many, many more.

Linkedin has many great aspects to it for real estate professionals, here are a few:

1. You profile will be found in google and the search engines so people can easily find you

2. You can ask and answer questions that are regularly indexed in the search engines and buyers & sellers read them regularly

3. You can share links, videos, and much more with your contacts and group members to view almost instantly

4. You can import your blogger using blog link and all your tweets from twitter to show up on your profile page

5. You can also list events you are having such as open houses, buyers seminars, etc. very easily and share it with all your connections

6. You can also promote your real estate services to the groups individually as let them know that you are available to serve them

7. You can also share articles and ezines articles published about you and your services

Linkedin is also available by your mobile cell phone or portable devices so you can stay connected all the time. As real estate professionals we are always on the go, set your profile up to be mobile, then if someone contacts you, you can respond almost immediately.

You can also advertise on Linkedin, go to:

www.**LinkedIn**.com/**advertising**
https://www.linkedin.com/directads/

Here you can learn all the powerful ways to market your real estate services to investors and other business professionals in your community and globally.

Chapter 17
Trulia-A Very Powerful Website for Real Estate Professionals-A Must in Real Estate Marketing & Social Networking

What Is Trulia?

Trulia is a real estate search engine that helps buyers find homes for sale, real estate professionals, and provides real estate information at the local level. You can also connect with local real estate agents, realtors, and professionals in your area. Best of all you can market your real estate services!!

Buyers, investors, and sellers love Trulia and you should too! Your profile on Trulia will come up very good in the search engines and help people find and locate the services you have to offer. You can create blogs on Trulia also; many blogs on Trulia come up #1 or in the top searches on the search engines, what better way to advertise what you have to offer by creating free blogs. Trulia is also a tool for real estate professionals to market their listings, view real estate data and promote their services. If you are a broker or real estate agent, sign up to be listed in the Real Estate Professional's section.

Join Today & Create Your Profile On Trulia

www.trulia.com

Buyers and Sellers Love Trulia and You Should Too!
What trulia can do for you and your real estate business:

1. It's free to join and network!

2. Your profile will be found very easily in the search engines

3. You can create blogs about you, your area, or just about anything you would like to blog about to attrack buyers, sellers, and investors

4. You can ask questions and answer questions, many of trulia's question and ask forums come up in the Top 5 places of google and when you answer these questions buyers and sellers will see you and your profile, as well as they can contact you to request your services

5. You will appear to be a leader in your community gaining you much more business

6. You can share your profile and blogs in google and all the search engines so they can be found very easily

7. You can also upgrade your profile to pro status, they do charge a membership for the pro status but you will receive buyer and seller leads in your area of choice

8. You can also use trulia on the go, there is tulia mobile

9. Another new feature they have is called trulia local, for a fee you can be showcased as the local real estate pro in your area, fees do apply but this is a great way to reach people searching a specific area

10. Search and add widgets to your profile to further enhance the people reading your profiles

To learn all about the ways you can advertise and market directly on trulia, go to:
http://www.trulia.com/advertisers/

Chapter 18
Zillow-This is another Top Website to Join for Real Estate Professionals

What is Zillow?

Zillow.com is a one of the leading online real estate marketplaces dedicated to helping homeowners, buyers, sellers, renters, real estate agents, mortgage professionals, landlords, and property managers find and share vital information about homes, real estate, and mortgages.

Zillow's goal is to help people make intelligent decisions about their homes - whether it's buying a home, selling, renting, leasing, remodeling or financing - it's all about empowering people with data and information. Zillow is a great resource for Realtors.

What Zillow Does

When Zillow launched in early 2006, Zestimate home values were the cornerstone of the zillow website and quite revolutionary in their quest to create a database of all U.S. homes, whether they are for sale or not.

Since then, Zillow has rapidly grown to become one of the most comprehensive and most-visited Web sites for real estate and homes on the internet.

In addition to information and data on nearly all homes in the U.S., Zillow visitors can search homes for sale, homes for rent, recently sold homes, Make Me Move homes and more, as well as find mortgage solutions on Zillow Mortgage Marketplace and most importantly find local real estate agents "Realtors" in their area. Potential buyers and sellers can find a professional in the real estate directory or ask questions and find answers in Zillow Advice. You, the real estate professional can answer questions for these buyers and sellers and offer your expertise. And homeowners can browse remodeling ideas in Dueling Digs, or dig into the latest real estate trends in their neighborhood via Zillow's expansive local data pages.

Zillow is a media business model and makes money selling advertising and connecting homeowners, renters, buyers and sellers with professionals who can help them.

Zillow is a great place for Real Estate Professionals and you should be listed on Zillow. 12.5 Million People Use Zillow regularly.

To Join Zillow you will need to visit the website below and start by creating your profile, go to:
www.zillow.com

Once you have created your profile, add your profile picture and all contact information so people can get contact you and request your services. Next, make sure to add all areas you want to be listed in, the geographical areas you want to be found in. Then, go and make sure you are listed in the zillow directory.

It is free to join and network on zillow and thousands of buyers and sellers regularly use this real estate website to find properties, real estate agents & brokers, and find answers to all their real estate questions. You can also pay additional fees to be a Zillow Pro agent or broker, zillow will then send you buyer or seller leads, you can even specify which you would like or both.

To Learn All About the Different Ways you can advertise on Zillow,
Go to: http://www.zillow.com/advertising/

Chapter 19
ActiveRain-This is an amazing social network for Real Estate Agents & Brokers! This site is definitely a Must-Do in our category for becoming one of the Top Dogs in Social Media and Networking!

Go to:
http://activerain.com/

The ActiveRain Network hosts over 170,000 Real Estate Industry members averaging 200-300 new members daily. There are more than 1.5 million articles posted, with an average of 700-1000 new posts daily. Two million+ visitors traffic the ActiveRain network each month, over 80% are consumers. Only Rainmaker upgraded accounts receive Google traffic to their blogs and posts. ActiveRain Member's Blog posts receive more than 500 views on average. Activerain is the ONLY on-line Network that offers this wide variety of tools, diverse services, and proven solutions to the Real Estate Industry Professional and for consumers on the WEB.

Siging up with activerain is very easy, just simply fill in your contact information and you are on your way. If you need more help getting started, visit this website, it helps you step by step through the process of becoming an activerain member:
http://activerain.com/blogsview/1135403/how-to-get-started-on-activerain

Activerain started in 2006, but has become a very powerful resource for real estate professionals. The blogs posted on activerain commonly come up #1 or in the Top 5 of google searches! Once you join, completely fill out your profile and all contact information, then start answering questions and creating blogs. These blogs and forum question and answers on activerain get thousands of people reading them each and every day. Always include all your contact information and a link to your website so your next home buyer or homeseller can contact you right away!

The basic membership is free, they do offer upgraded memberships. We recommend to start with the free membership, then once you are registered with all your social networking websites and posting regularly, consider upgrading to the higher membership level. This site gives you great benefits either way and should be one of the top social networking websites to join!

Become a Rain Maker and Join ActiveRain Today!

Chapter 20
Biggerpockets-An Excellent Source for Investors for the Real Estate Professional

Biggerpockets is another top website where real estate pros can grow their business quickly. Real Estate investors love this site! Nearly 60,000 users are on biggerpockets.com and the bulk of them are investors. If you are looking to connect with investors, this is one of the best websites for you. Investors are great clients to have as they repeatedly buy and sell homes compared to the normal homeowner who only moves every so often.

Join Biggerpockets.com today!
Go to:
http://www.biggerpockets.com/

Once you have created your profile on biggerpockets, add your photos and all contact information about yourself. You can quickly create blogs and connect with people on this website, as well as join large groups of people. Join as many groups as possible, when you first sign up there is usually a limit of 20 groups you can join, however once you have started networking regularly you can easily start adding more groups.

You can also place ads and advertise directly on biggerpockets, go to the link below and learn about all the great ways you can advertise your Real Estate Services on Biggerpockets:
http://www.biggerpockets.com/advertise

Chapter 21
Foreclosure Network-It's Free to Join and Network with Buyers, Sellers, Investors, and other Real Estate Professionals

This is a great site as buyers love to buy foreclosures! It's free to join and network and this website is growing very rapidly. It is one very upcoming website focused on foreclosures and the foreclosure industry.

Join today! Go to:
www.foreclosurecleanupnetwork.com

Here you can create a very customize profile of yourself and your real estate services, create blogs, ask and answer questions, contact buyers and sellers directly through this site and it's all free. You can also add widgets to your profile and instantly share your information to facebook, Google, twitter, and much more!

Chapter 22
Google Profiles-Be Instantly Found in Google With your Own Profile Directly on Google

Very few Real Estate Agents and Realtors use this free top marketing tool, however this can quickly get you found on the first page of Google and quickly help you achieve a lot of visitors for your blogs, facebook, and much more. To sign up and create your free Google profile, go to:

www.google.com/profiles

Your Google profile will come up when people Google search your name or local area. It will display all of your contact information as well as you can add links to your facebook, twitter, myspace, blogs, your website, and any other links you would like to add. Always make sure to add a profile picture of yourself as people love to view profiles with pictures. You can also add links to videos you have posted on YouTube and much, much more!

Chapter 23
Blogger-Blogger is one of the Best Places to Write and Post Blogs on the Internet

Blogger is free and a great source to be used by all Real Estate Agents and Realtors. You can set up your blogger account very quickly and immediately start posting blogs about you, your services, your local area, and anything you would like to blog about.

Go to:
www.blogger.com and create your free account now. If you have a Google or gmail email account, just enter that log in and start blogging!

This is a great blogging platform and it run by Google so your blogs will easily be indexed in the Google search. It has completely customizable templates for your blogs and you can even earn money on your blogs by using Google adsense.

Chapter 24
Google Buzz-Similar to Twitter, but From Google

Now that you have a Google account, add Google buzz to your profile and every blog or update you post to your profile can immediately be shared on Google buzz.

Go to: http://www.google.com/buzz

You can also share from other websites to Google buzz and it provides Real-time instant status updates of what you are posting just like twitter does.

You can share pictures, videos, ezine article links, blog links, website links, and just about anything you would like to share on google buzz and because google owns it, it will be found on the google search very well!

Chapter 25
Wordpress- One of the Top Blogging Platforms on the Internet

Wordpress is a great blogging tool and necessity for Real Estate professionals or literally any business!

The best part of wordpress is google and the search engines love it and index these blogs very, very high! Most people traditionally when searching for properties or information on the internet only click on the first 5 items that comes up in the search results. If you are not found in the top 5 results, most likely the peson will not ever reach your website and contact you.

What is Wordpress?
WordPress started in 2003 with a single bit of code to enhance the typography of everyday writing and with fewer users than you can count on your fingers and toes. Since then it has grown to be the largest self-

hosted blogging tool in the world, used on millions of sites and seen by tens of millions of people every day. On this site you can download and install a software script called WordPress. To do this you need a web host who meets the minimum requirements and a little time. WordPress is completely customizable and can be used for almost anything.

There is also a service called WordPress.com which lets you get started with a new and free WordPress-based blog in seconds, but varies in several ways and is less flexible than the WordPress you download and install yourself.

What Can You Use WordPress For?

WordPress started as just a blogging system, but has evolved to be used as full content management system and so much more through the thousands of plug-ins, widgets, and themes; WordPress is limited only by your imagination.

Key Features of WordPress:

WordPress Offers Full standards compliance — They have gone to great lengths to make sure that every bit of WordPress generated code is in full compliance with the standards of theW3C. This is important not only for interoperability with today's browser but also for forward compatibility with the tools of the next generation. Most importantly WordPress blogs come up top in most of the search engines!!! This is what you are looking for, remember the more people that find you online the more clients you will get. Thus the more commissions you will earn per year! Always remember your goal is total internet domination! The more places you are found and content out there about you and your services, the more easily it will be for you to dominate your local real estate market on the web. WordPress feels your web site is a beautiful thing, and you should demand nothing less.

No rebuilding — Changes you make to your templates or entries are reflected immediately on your site, with no need for regenerating static pages.

WordPress Pages — Pages allow you to manage non-blog content easily, so for example you could have a static "About" page that you manage through WordPress. For an idea of how powerful this is, the entire WordPress.org site could be run off WordPress alone.

WordPress Links -- Links allow you to create, maintain, and update any number of blogrolls through your administration interface. This is much faster than calling an external blogroll manager.

WordPress Themes — WordPress comes with a full theme system which makes designing everything from the simplest blog to the most complicated webzine a piece of cake, and you can even have multiple themes with totally different looks that you switch with a single click. Have a new design every day.

Cross-blog communication tools— WordPress fully supports both the Trackback and Pingback standards, and we are committed to supporting future standards as they develop.

Comments — Visitors to your site can leave comments on individual entries and through Trackback or Pingback can comment on their own site. You can enable or disable comments on a per-post basis.

Spam protection — Out of the box WordPress comes with very robust tools such as an integrated blacklist and open proxy checker to manage and eliminate comment spam on your blog, and there is also a rich array of plug-ins that can take this functionality a step further.

Full user registration — WordPress has a built-in user registration system that (if you choose) can allow people to register and maintain profiles and leave authenticated comments on your blog. You can optionally close comments for non-registered users. There is also plug-ins that hide posts from lower level users.

Password Protected Posts — You can give passwords to individual posts to hide them from the public. You can also have private posts which are viewable only by their author.

Easy installation and upgrades — Installing WordPress and upgrading from previous versions and other software is a piece of cake. Try it and you'll wonder why all web software isn't this easy.

Workflow — You can have types of users that can only post drafts, not publish to the front page such as your assistant or partner.

Intelligent text formatting — If you've dealt with systems that convert new lines to line breaks before you know why they have a bad name: if you have any sort of HTML they butcher it by putting tags after every new line indiscriminately, breaking your formatting and validation. Our function for this intelligently avoids places where you already have breaks and block-level HTML tags, so you can leave it on without worrying about it breaking your code.

Multiple authors — WordPress' highly advanced user system allows up to 10 levels of users, with different levels having different (and configurable) privileges with regard to publishing, editing, options, and other users.

Bookmarklets — Cross-browser bookmarklets make it easy to publish to your blog or add links to your blogroll with a minimum of effort.

Ping away — WordPress supports pinging Ping-O-Matic, which means maximum exposure for your blog to search engines.

Go to: http://wordpress.org/

Now to start your own WordPress blog, post regularly to your blog; also make sure to list it on your blogger blog, your website, and any other websites and social networking sites you belong to. This will help drive traffic to your websites and also give you great links back to your main website.

Other Great Blogging Websites to Try are:
ExpressionEngine, LiveJournal, Open Diary, TypePad, Vox, Xanga

Some Good Microblogging Websites are:

FMyLife, Foursquare, Jaiku, Plurk, Posterous, Tumblr, Twitter, Qaiku, Yammer, Google Buzz

Chapter 26

Yelp- This is a place where customers or past clients can post reviews on your real estate services and about you.

Yelp is a very powerful marketing tool to use and should be used by all Real Estate Professionals.

Yelp comes up near the very top of Google and most search engines!! Be found quickly with yelp.

Go to: http://www.yelp.com/ to create your own yelp account.

Start out by posting any and all testimonials you have received and post them all on yelp. You will look like the leader in the community and it will drive tons of internet traffic to your website page and hopefully in turn bring you much, much business.

Some statistics on yelp:

In the last 30 days 38 Million people visited yelp and the numbers are growing rapidly!

Yelpers have written over *12 million* local reviews, 83% of them rating a business 3 stars or higher.

In addition to reviews, you can use Yelp to find events, special offers, lists and to talk with other Yelpers.

You can Yelp on your phone at http://m.yelp.com, or use Yelp for iPhone, Yelp for BlackBerry, Yelp for Palm Pre, and Yelp for Android.

You can also pay to advertise directly on Yelp.

Visit yelp.com today to get your real estate services noticed quickly!

Chapter 27
PING.FM-This Tool will make your life as an internet marketer and social media giant a cinch!

What is Ping.fm?

Ping.fm is a simple and FREE service that makes updating your social networks a snap! On Ping.fm you will create a free account and then enter all of your user profile logins and passwords, then any blog, website, article, video, pictures, etc you want to post on the internet can be posted in this one location and immediately posted on ALL of your social media networking websites.

Now that you have created accounts on many social networking websites, Ping.fm makes posting to all of these websites at one time a cinch. You will need to create your free account on Ping.fm, and then enter all of your usernames and passwords into Ping.fm. Then, you can just log in daily and post on Ping.fm and your post will automatically be submitted to your facebook page, myspace, linkedin, twitter, and so many more.

To get started using ping.fm right away, Go to: www.ping.fm

This is one of the best tools on the web! There may also be other social networking sharing websites, however we have used this one extensively and it is very easy and user friendly to use.

Sharing Social Media Across the Web Instantly

There is another great tool to utilize that allows you to literally share any webpage on all of the social media and networking websites almost instantly including your own website.

It's called social bookmarking share.
Here are a couple of websites that offer this:
www.addthis.com
www.addtoany.com

www.sharethis.com
http://www.socialmarker.com/

Many of these websites have tool bars you can download right to your own computer and instantly share any articles, blogs, or WebPages all over the internet with real-time results. And there are many, many more!!

To take advantage of using these services, just create a free profile and usually you will download their toolbar onto your computer, so websites allow you to do it straight from there website but you will benefit much more by having it directly on your web browser, then any website, blog, video, or webpage you would like to share and submit to the search engines you can with just the click of the mouse.

Also, when you create new blogs and content, this allows you to get the new content shared almost instantly with Google, Yahoo, Bing, and all the other search engines as well as other social networking websites such as delicious, digg, and many more websites. Currently add this allows you to share on nearly 800 websites and growing daily.

What an amazingly great way to have your information, websites, blogs, and social networking websites show up all over the internet!

We highly recommend using these advanced sharing techniques! This is THE best way to quickly distribute your content all over the internet very, very quickly. Nearly every website you go to has this capability, but is rarely used by real estate agents. Just creating good content is not the most important task; it's having people find it online. With sharing tools bars and widgets, this is now very easy!!

Chapter 28
Social Media Using Videos-The Way of the Future

Create Videos and Post Them To Myspace, Facebook, YouTube, & Many other Websites offering your Real Estate Services

YouTube Traffic and Stats

People are watching 2 billion videos a day on YouTube and uploading hundreds of thousands of videos daily. In fact, every minute, 24 hours of video is uploaded to YouTube.

Demographics of YouTube Visitors

You Tube's user base is broad in age range, 18-55, evenly divided between males and females, and spanning all geographies. Fifty-one percent of our users go to YouTube weekly or more often, and 52 percent of 18-34 year-olds share videos often with friends and colleagues. With such a large and diverse user base, YouTube offers something for everyone. YouTube is now the #2 search place for content on the internet, and it is now also owned by Google. This meaning videos uploaded on YouTube will be probably be indexed in Google very well and this is our goal. Many times videos show up in the first 5 search results for Google once they have been indexed.

Advertising on YouTube

Marketers have embraced the YouTube marketing platform and as an innovative and engaging vehicle for connecting with their target audiences and they are increasing sales and exposure for their companies and brands in many different ways. In some cases, they run video advertising, such as InVideo Ads or YouTube video ads, but they are also sponsoring contests, creating brand channels, and adding their own original content to the site. This model is a natural fit for the YouTube community because it follows one of the general philosophies of the site itself—user experience comes first. YouTube's community has defined what works in this space, and we'll continue to innovate based on their feedback.

There are several other ways for users, partners, and advertisers to benefit from engaging with the millions of people who make up the world's largest online video community:

YouTube Insight: A free tool offered by YouTube that allows anyone with a YouTube account—users, partners, or advertisers—to view detailed statistics about the videos that they upload to the site.

The YouTube Partner Program: Original content creators have the chance to generate revenue from their work and receive the same promotional benefits afforded to YouTube's other professional content partners.

You can learn about advertising on YouTube by visiting their own brand channel:
YouTube and Google

YouTube is an independent subsidiary of Google Inc., having been acquired by the leader in search and online advertising services in November of 2006.

Google and YouTube share the vision of enabling anyone to find, upload, watch and share original videos worldwide, and the dedication to innovate with video to offer compelling services for our users and for content owners.

Embrace YouTube and Creating Videos, this is truly the way of the future. People love pictures, but they love videos even more! Plus it is a great way to drive traffic to your website or get those buyers and sellers to contact you as you can also post all of your contact information right next to the videos you upload and post.

Creating a video is relatively easy in this day and age, you can even do it from a lot of cell phones and post your video in minutes. Create videos advertising your expertise and what you have to offer and then upload your video to YouTube, myspace, and facebook with links back to your website so your potential customers can find you.

Nearly all new digital cameras even have a feature to take video and it can easily be uploaded to YouTube and multiple video websites.

Google loves video and being google owns YouTube, you have a very good chance your videos that are posted on YouTube will show up in the google search results as well as other search engines. This can bring a windfall of traffic to your website and make it very easy to find you and your Real Estate Services online.

When you have created a video, YouTube is the place to start. Go to: http://www.youtube.com/

Create a free account and upload your video or videos, you can even create a channel dedicated to your local area and post all your videos to this channel.

Make sure to include keywords to your new video so it can easily be indexed into the search engines.

You can also place ads of YouTube to attract visitors to your website.

To learn how you can advertise on YouTube, go to: www.youtube.com/t/advertising

Chapter 29
Video Sharing-Blast Your Videos All Over the Internet Quickly

Just like how you were able to share you blogs, website, and other social networking websites all over the internet, you can blast your videos everywhere too!

There are several video sharing websites similar to how Ping.fm works for submitting normal blogs, websites, and content.

Here are some of the Video Sharing Websites you can post your videos on to blast them all over the internet:
sevenload, Viddler, Vimeo, YouTube, Dailymotion, Metacafe, Nico Nico Douga, Openfilm, TubeMogul

Chapter 30
Publish Free Articles About Yourself, Your Area, and Your Community

You can actually **create and publish free articles** and submit them all over the web about yourself, your community and more.
Website links to publish ezine articles and press releases:

www.webpronews.com

www.webknowhow.net

www.thewhir.com

www.marketingsource.com

www.buzzle.com

www.members.ezinearticles.com

www.isnare.com

www.goarticles.com

www.articleclick.com

Website links to publish ezine articles and press releases continued:

www.threadwatch.org

www.qarchive.org

www.articlecity.com

www.articlebiz.com

www.webmasterbrain.com

www.devpointer.net

www.articledashboard.com

www.allmerchants.com

www.bharatbhasha.com

www.selfseo.com

www.searchwarp.com

www.articlealley.com

www.marketing-seek.com

Website links to publish ezine articles and press releases continued:

www.workoninternet.com

www.articleblast.com

www.articledepot.co.uk

www.articlesphere.com

www.articleworld.net

www.free-articles-zone.com

www.expertarticles.com

www.businesshighlight.org

www.amazines.com

www.articleson.com

www.members.article99.com

www.articlemarketer.com

www.seoarticles4u.com

Website links to publish ezine articles and press releases Continued:

www.workathomearticles.net

www.morganarticlearchive.com

www.articlebin.com

www.article-content-king.com

www.articlesbeyondbetter.com

www.articlegeek.com

www.a1articles.com

www.valuablecontent.com

www.media13.com

www.submityournewarticle.com

www.reprintedarticles.com

www.article-spot.com

Chapter 31
Free Classified Ads for Real Estate Tons of Websites You Can Place **Free** Classified Ads Offering Your Real Estate Services On & Market Your Listings

www.usfreeads.com

www.inetgiant.com

www.classifiedsforfree.com

www.webcosmo.com

www.freeadsplanet.com

www.freeadlists.com

www.thefreeadforum.com

www.postadsdaily.com

www.porkypost.com

www.global-free-classified-ads.com

www.freeadvertisingblog.com

www.adjingo.com

www.adsglobe.com

www.craigslist.org

www.kijiji.com

www.backpage.com

FREE Classified Ad Websites:

www.kaango.com

www.oodle.com

www.olx.com

www.economist.com/Classifieds/

www.classifieds.myspace.com/

www.classifiedads.com/

www.domesticsale.com/

www.traderonline.com/

www.google.com/base

www.adlandpro.com/

www.adpost.com/

www.ebayclassifieds.com/

www.inetgiant.com/

www.latimes.com/classified/

www.hoobly.com/

www.house.info/home.php

www.uscity.net/

www.recycler.com/

www.sell.com/

www.bestwayclassifieds.com

FREE Classified Ad Websites:

www.classifiedclub.com

www.50statesclassifieds.com

www.ablewise.com

www.isell.com/

www.stumblehere.com/

www.5starads.com/post_ads.html

www.freeadpost.com/

www.phinditt.com/

www.usnetads.com/

www.walmart.oodle.com/

www.webclassifieds.us/

www.beatyourprice.com/

www.wantadsonline.com/

www.sandpointonline.com/

www.eyeone.com/

www.wantedwants.com/

www.tampaonlineclassifieds.com/

www.nj.com/classifieds/free/

www.theadnet.com/

www.lehighvalleylive.com/classifieds/free/

FREE Classified Ad Websites:

www.informationex.com/

www.jeffcity.net/web/index.htm

www.nola.com/classifieds/free/

www.oregonlive.com/classifieds/free/

www.buckeyeads.com/

www.jihoy.com/

www.al.com/classifieds/free/

www.mlive.com/classifieds/free/

www.freesearching.com/classified_ad.htm

www.webpagepublicity.com/free-classified-ads.html

www.familiesonlinemagazine.com/classifieds.html

www.classifiedflyerads.com/

www.mixmarket.com/

www.freeadvertisingexchange.com/

www.enoun.com/

www.masslive.com/classifieds/free/

www.ad.gogopin.com/

www.iwanna.com/

www.yardsalenet.net/

www.metrowny.com/ads.php

Chapter 32
Internet Marketing Tools for Advertising Your Listings

Free Property Video Creator
http://www.propertypreviews.com

Multiple Free Webpage Listing Submission
http://www.postlets.com
http://www.VFlyers.com
http://www.threewide.com

Free Single Listing Pages
http://www.RealBird.com

Free Virtual Tours Online
http://www.propertypreviews.com
http://www.homezonemedia.com

Electronic Newsletter
http://www.myemma.com
http://www.verticalresponse.com

Client Management Services for Real Estate

Free Contact Real Estate Contact Management Software
http://www.realfuturecrm.com/public/

Tools for Photos and Graphics
Free Photo Management / Editing & Alterating Photos & Graphics
http://www.picnik.com
http://picasa.google.com/
http://www.Flickr.com
http://www.photobucket.com

Free Open source Image Software (like Photoshop)
http://www.gimp.org/

Photo Tools and Resources
http://www.Flickr.com
http://www.CreativeCommons.org
http://www.greedigitalphotos.net
http://www.frephoto1.com
http://www.freephotosbank.com

Free Presentation Sharing
http://www.slideshare.net

Satellite Photos
http://earth.google.com
http://www.google.com/maps

Research and Reference

National Association of Realtors
http://www.realtor.org/library

Address and Telephone Number:
http://www.anywho.com/

CLUE Choice Trust (Home Owner Insurance Reports)
http://www.choicetrust.com

CIA Worldfact Books
www.cia.gov/cia/publications/factbook/index.html

Real Estate Market Information
http://www.restats.com
http://altosresearch.com/

Remodeling Value Report
http://www.costvsvalue.com/southatlantic.html

Market Research
http://www.realtor.org/research
http://www.housingmarketfacts.com/

Time Zone Converter
http://www.timeanddate.com/worldclock/meeting.html

Calculate What Their Rent Will Buy
http://www.mortgage-calc.com/index.html

Census Bureau
www.census.gov

City/State/HUD Websites Permits
http://Socds.huduser.org/permits/index.html

Use American Fact Finder to find demographic
information
http://factfinder.census.gov/home/saff/main.html?_lang=en

Bureau of Labor and Statistics
http://www.bls.gov/oes/current/oessrcma.htm

City Sites
http://www.citysearch.com/

Weather Sites
www.nws.noaa.gov
www.bestplaces.net/climate/

Crime statistics
www.fbi.gov
www.fedstats.gov

www.bestplaces.net/crime/
Free Demographics
http://www.freedemographics.com/

Date Calculator:
http://www.timeanddate.com/date/dateadd.html

Credit Score and Information
http://www.myfico.com
http://www.AnnualCreditReport.com

National Do Not Call
https://telemarketing.donotcall.gov/

Bandwidth Test
http://bandwidthplace.com/speedtest/

Google Maps
http://www.google.com/maps
http://www.mapquest.com/

School Report Cards
http://www.GreatSchools.net

EPA Model Guide
http://www.epa.gov/mold/moldresources.html

EPA Radon Guide
http://www.p2pays.org/ref/17/radon/pubs/hmbyguid.html

EPA Lead Based Paint Booklet
http://www.epa.gov/lead/pubs/leadpdfe.pdf

GREEN Tools for Real Estate

Walkability of a House Location
http://www.WalkScore.com

Environmental Protection Agency
http://www.epa.gov/

Smart Growth Resources
http://www.smartgrowth.org

Green Real Estate Remodeling Guidelines
http://www.regreenprogram.org/documents/regreen_g
uidelines.pdf

RE Green Program
http://www.regreenprogram.org

NAR GREEN Council
http://www.greenresourcecouncil.org/

HUD FHA Energy Efficient Mortgage
http://www.hud.gov/offices/hsg/sfh/eem/energy-r.cfm

REALTOR® Tools

NRDS Number Locator
www.NRDS.InternetCrusade.com

REALTOR® Resources
www.REALTOR.org

Webpage Tools
Website Focus Group Info
http://www.clickdensity.com

Free Webpage Analytics
http://www.google.com/analytics
http://www.visistat.com

Create Maps to Put on Your Site
http://www.zeemaps.com

Free Flash Website Creator
http://www.wix.com/

Meta Tag Designer
www.submitshop.com/metatags/metatags.html

Compare Google Search Terms
http://google.com/insights

Widget for webpage that allows communication with
Instant Messaging
http://www.hab.la/

Google Search Engine Optimization Guidelines
www.google.com/webmasters/docs/search-engine-
optimization-starter-guide.pdf

Google Webmaster tools
https://www.google.com/webmasters/tools

Open Directory Project SEO Tool
http://www.dmoz.org/

Tools to Grow Your Real Estate Blogs & Website
http://www.MyBlogLog.com
http://www.Google.com/reader
http://www.RealEstateTomato.com
http://www.RSSPieces.com

Free Hosting (no ads)
http://www.FreeHostia.com

Free or Inexpensive Blog Systems
http://www.Wordpress.com
http://www.Typepad.com
http://www.Blogger.com
http://www.Activerain.com/outsideblogs

Video Tools

Free webcam / streaming Video software
http://www.yawcam.com

Free Video, Chat and VOIP Services
http://www.Skype.com
http://www.TokBox.com

On-Line Videos
www.YouTube.com
www.tubemogul.com

Video Distribution
http://www.vimeo.com
http://www.wellcomemat.com
http://www.mlbroadcast.com

http://www.turnhere.com
Free iPOD Conversion and Hosting
http://www.Podbean.com

Free Video Capture Tool
http://www.Screen-o-matic.com

Online Meeting Tools

Free Online Meeting Software
http://www.yugma.com

Free Conference Call
http://www.freeconferencecall.com

Meeting Scheduling
http://www.MeetingWizard.com

Group Meeting Scheduling Tool
http://www.timebridge.com

Communication Tools

Instant Communication Tools
http://www.meebo.com/
http://www.Skype.com
http://www.Digsby.com

E-Mail Business Card
http://www.emailideas.com/

SMS Messaging Service
http://smseverywhere.com/send.htm

Free Voice to E-mail systems
http://www.Jott.com
http://www.rememberthemilk.com

Send a message that automatically deletes after receipt
https://privnote.com/

Fax to Email System
www.MaxEmail.com
www.efax.com

Document Management

On-Line Document Management
http://www.DocStoc.com

Online Document Storage & Backup Services
http://www.Carbonite.com
http://www.documentree.com

http://www.box.net
http://mozy.com/

Send Large Files (All files under 100mb)
http://goaruna.com/

Print anything to PDF, without Adobe (Free)
http://www.cutepdf.com/
www.Primopdf.com

Additional Services

Open Source Office Applications
www.OpenOffice.org
http://www.google.com/apps
http://www.campfirenow.com/
http://www.thinkfree.com
http://www.zoho.com

Social Media

Social Media Bookmarking Websites
http://www.del.icio.us.com
http://www.sharethis.com
http://www.friendfeed.com
http://www.MyBlogLog.com
http://www.retagger.com

Micro-Blogging
http://www.Twitter.com
http://www.google.com/buzz

Social Media Websites for Real Estate
http://www.Facebook.com
http://www.MySpace.com
http://www.Twitter.com
http://www.zillow.com/
http://activerain.com/
http://www.trulia.com/
http://www.yelp.com/
http://www.biggerpockets.com/

On-Line Networking and Resume Sites
http://www.Plaxo.com
http://www.linkedin.com

Widgets
Twitter Follow Widgets
http://twitbuttons.com/

Area Schools Widget
http://www.education.com/schoolfinder/tools/localschools-widget/

Misc. Tools
E-Signatures or Digital Electronic Signatures
http://www.docusign.com
http://www.echosign.com

Zipforms
www.ZipForms.com

Google Help:
www.Google.pack.com

Free USB Office Tools
http://www.xtort.net/office-and-productivity/floppy-office/

REALTOR® On-Line Tools

Neighborhood Tours
http://www.maps.google.com
http://www.everyscape.com

Real Estate News
Real Estate Industry News
http://www.Inman.com
http://www.RealtyTimes.com
http://www.RisMedia.com
http://www.BrokerAgentNews.com

All these tools can be implemented into your advertising campaigns and require very little money on your part!! Invest your time and you will be successful in your real estate business. Internet is the way of the future and real estate professionals that market on the internet usually dominate their market area! Make your potential customers find your website and request your services, quit paying for leads. Start generating good, viable leads from your own website. You pay for your website month after month, make it start paying you in rewards with leads!!!

This is your business-Take charge of your business now and get found online!!! There are real estate professionals generating 10-100 leads per month from their website!!! You can too!

We wish you much success in becoming a Real Estate Internet Giant!! Get started now so people can start finding you and using your services!!

For More Great Real Estate Training & Tools,

Go to: www.DreamStreetInvestments.com

Chapter 33
Internet & Online Definitions

Autoresponder: An autoresponder is a program or script on a mail server that automatically replies to e-mails. Though it is run from the mail server, an autoresponder can usually be set up by the user through a Web-based interface. For example, a company might set up an autoresponder for their support e-mail address to let users know they have received their support requests. The automated reply might read something like, "Thank you, we have received your message.

Blog: Short for "Web Log," this term refers to a list of journal entries posted on a Web page. Anybody who knows how to create and publish a Web page can publish their own blog. Some Web hosts have made it even easier by creating an interface where users can simply type a text entry and hit "publish" to publish their blog.

Bookmark: Similar to a real-life bookmark, an Internet bookmark acts as a marker for a Web site. (In Internet Explorer, they're called "Favorites".) When using a Web browser, you can simply select a bookmark from the browser's Bookmarks menu to go to a certain site. This way, you don't have to go through the redundant process of typing in the Internet address each time you visit one of your favorite sites.

Domain Name: This is the name that identifies a Web site. For example, "microsoft.com" is the domain name of Microsoft's Web site. A single Web server can serve Web sites for multiple domain names, but a single domain name can point to only one machine.

Email: It's hard to remember what our lives were like without e-mail. Ranking up there with the Web as one of the most useful features of the Internet, e-mail has become one of today's standard means of communication. Common email provides are gmail, yahoo mail, there are literally hundreds of email providers available.

Home Page: This is the starting point or front page of a Web site. This page usually has some sort of table of contents on it and often describes the purpose of the site.

HTML (Hyper-Text Markup Language): Stands for "Hyper-Text Markup Language." This is the language that Web pages are written in. Also known as hypertext documents, Web pages must conform to the rules of HTML in order to be displayed correctly in a Web browser. The HTML syntax is based on a list of tags that describe the page's format and what is displayed on the Web page.

IP Address: Also known as an "IP number" or simply an "IP," this is a code made up of numbers separated by three dots that identifies a particular computer on the Internet. Every computer, whether it be a Web server or the computer you're using right now, requires an IP address to connect to the Internet. IP addresses consist of four sets of numbers from 0 to 255, separated by three dots. For example "66.72.98.236" or "216.239.115.148". Your Internet Service Provider (ISP), will assign you either a static IP address (which is always the same) or a dynamic IP address, (which changes every time you log on). ISPs typically assign dial-up users a dynamic IP address each time they sign on because it reduces the number of IP addresses they must register.

JavaScript: Like Java, this is a programming language designed by Sun Microsystems, in conjunction with Netscape that can be integrated into standard HTML pages. While JavaScript is based on the Java syntax, it is a scripting language, and therefore cannot be used to create stand-alone programs. Instead, it is used mainly to create dynamic, interactive Web pages

Link: When you are browsing the Web and you see a highlighted and underlined word or phrase on a page, there is a good chance you are looking at a link. By clicking on a link, you can "jump" to a new Web page or a completely different Web site. While text links are typically blue and underlined, they can be any color and don't have to be underlined. Images can also serve as links to other Web pages. When you move the cursor over a link in a Web page, the arrow will turn into a little hand, letting you know that it is a link. The term "hypertext" comes from the way links can quickly send you to another Web destination.

Meta Tags: This is a special HTML tag that is used to store information about a Web page but is not displayed in a Web browser. For example, Meta tags provide information such as what program was used to create the page, a description of the page, and keywords that are relevant to the page. Many search engines use the information stored in Meta tags when they index Web pages.

RSS: Stands for "RDF Site Summary," but is commonly referred to as "Really Simple Syndication." RSS is method of providing website content such as news stories or software updates in a standard XML format.

Search Engine: Google, Excite, Lycos, AltaVista, Infoseek, Bing, and Yahoo are all search engines. They index millions of sites on the Web, so that Web surfers like you and me can easily find Web sites with the information we want. By creating indexes, or large databases of Web sites (based on titles, keywords, and the text in the pages), search engines can locate relevant Web sites when users enter search terms or phrases. When you are looking for something using a search engine, it is a good idea to use words like AND, OR, and NOT to specify your search.

SEO (Search Engine Optimization): Stands for "Search Engine Optimization." Just about every Webmaster wants his or her site to appear in the top listings of all the major search engines.

SMM (Social Media Marketing): Stands for "Social Media Marketing." SMM refers to marketing done through social media or social networking websites. While most companies and organizations have their own websites, it can be difficult to reach users who do not already know about the organization. Social media marketing provides a low cost way for businesses to reach large numbers of users and gain brand recognition. Since social networking websites already have large established online communities, businesses and organizations can gain exposure by simply joining these websites. Organizations can create custom social media profiles, and then build their own communities within these sites by adding users as friends or followers.

Social Networking: Social networking websites allow users to be part of a virtual community. The two most popular sites are currently Facebook and Myspace. These websites provide users with simple tools to create a custom profile with text and pictures. A typical profile includes basic information about the user, at least one photo, and possibly a blog or other comments published by the user. Advanced profiles may include videos, photo albums, online applications (in Facebook), or custom layouts (in Myspace). After creating a profile, users can add friends, send messages to other users, and leave comments directly on friends' profiles. These features provide the building blocks for creating online communities.

Spam: Sending direct email messages to the public to solicit the receiver without there previously approval.

Tweet: A tweet is an online posting, or micro-blog created by a Twitter user. The purpose of each tweet is to answer the question, "What are you doing?" However, tweets can contain any information you want to post, such as your plans for the weekend, your thoughts about a TV show, or even notes from a lecture. You can publish a tweet using a computer or a mobile phone. Once published, the tweet will appear on the Twitter home pages of all the users that are following you. Likewise, your Twitter home page will display the most recent tweets of the users that you are

following.
Each tweet is limited to 140 characters or less.

Url Address: This is the website address a web page is located at. Stands for "Uniform Resource Locator." A URL is the address of a specific Web site or file on the Internet. It cannot have spaces or certain other characters and uses forward slashes to denote different directories.

Web Browser: This is the browser you use to access the internet such as internet explorer, firefox, etc.

Web Host: In order to publish a website online, you need a Web host. The Web host stores all the pages of your website and makes them available to computers connected to the Internet. The domain name, such as "sony.com," is actually linked to an IP Address that points to a specific computer. When somebody enters your domain name into their browser's address field, the IP address is located and Web site is loaded from your Web host.

A Web host can have anywhere from one to several thousand computers that run Web hosting software, such as Apache, OS X Server, or Windows Server. Most websites you see on the Web are accessed from a "shared host," which is a single computer that can host several hundred Web sites. Larger websites often use a "dedicated host,"

141

which is a single machine that hosts only one website. Sites with extremely high amounts of traffic, such as apple.com or microsoft.com, use several computers to host one site.

If you want to publish your own website, you'll need to sign up for a "Web hosting service."

Web Page: Web pages are what make up the World Wide Web. These documents are written in HTML (hypertext markup language) and are translated by your Web browser. Web pages can either be static or dynamic. Static pages show the same content each time they are viewed. Dynamic pages have content that can change each time they are accessed. These pages are typically written in scripting languages such as PHP, Perl, ASP, or JSP. The scripts in the pages run functions on the server that return things like the date and time, and database information. All the information is returned as HTML code, so when the page gets to your browser, all the browser has to do is translate the HTML.

Please note that a Web page is not the same thing as a Web site. A Web site is a collection of pages. A Web page is an individual HTML document.

Website: A website, or Web site, is not the same thing as a Web page. Though the two terms are often used interchangeably, they should not be. So what's the difference? To put it simply, a Web site is a collection of Web pages. For example, Amazon.com is a Web site, but there are millions of Web pages that make up the site.

WWW "World Wide Web": Stands for "World Wide Web." It is important to know that this is not a synonym for the Internet. The World Wide Web, or just "the Web," as ordinary people call it, is a subset of the Internet. The Web consists of pages that can be accessed using a Web browser. The Internet is the actual network of networks where all the information resides. Things like Telnet, FTP, Internet gaming, Internet Relay Chat (IRC), and e-mail are all part of the Internet, but are not part of the World Wide Web. The Hyper-Text Transfer Protocol (HTTP) is the method used to transfer Web pages to your computer. With hypertext, a word or phrase can contain a link to another Web site. All Web pages are written in the hyper-text markup language (HTML), which works in conjunction with HTTP.

144

www.ingramcontent.com/pod-product-compliance
Lightning Source LLC
Chambersburg PA
CBHW071209050326
40689CB00011B/2282